LIFE BEHIND THE MASK

How Post Natal Depression Affected Me As a Man!

Richard Wharton

LIFE BEHIND THE MASK

By: Richard Wharton

RICH WHARTON

I dedicate this book to my incredible family. My Wife and my 2 amazing children who I completely adore! Thank you for being there for me through light and dark times!
I love you!

LIFE BEHIND THE MASK

Chapters

1. Introduction
2. Preface
3. My Story
4. Mental Health
5. Post Natal Depression
6. Friends & Family
7. Personal Development
8. Feeling Good
9. Charities & Support Partners

LIFE BEHIND THE MASK

Preface

This book is a tale of my story and some of the things I did to try and help myself.

This book is in no way here to diagnose, treat and linked with any medical suggestions to anyone.

If you are struggling or feel you need support with any Mental Health related issues, please seek medical advice through the appropriate channels or through a charity.

Appropriate channels include but not limited to: Your Doctors Surgery, NHS 111 service, Samaritans Charity, MIND – The Mental Health Charity and any other Mental Health Charity or Organisation.

Introduction

It's supposed to be the happiest moment of your life!

Welcoming your new son or daughter into this world, it's supposed to be the best feeling ever with so many positive emotions flowing. But it doesn't always work out like that for everyone…

For me, it was very very different! On the birth of my first child, it was incredible. The second, I felt completely different emotions.

The feelings of helplessness, feeling lost, sad and completely stressed were just some of the emotions I was feeling. Getting angry and calling my month old son all the names under the sun. Simply not being able to cope with being home alone with my boy, just because I knew that the crying would get to me.

I never had any feelings, thoughts or intentions of hurting my son or myself. I knew he would be perfectly safe and that I was "in control" of my emotions, but it still didn't stop the overwhelming feelings flood over me.

Why did I feel like this? What was different from the first to the second? What was happening to me?

There was one simple answer; I was suffering from Post Natal Depression.

My Story

My First Child was born in March 2017 – a beautiful girl.

In August 2021, my son was born - completing my incredible family.

Being a Father of 2 is something special, a daughter and a son, both natural births with no real difficulties through the whole pregnancy and post birth. My Wife and I were so lucky and privileged to have everything perfect. Yes there were moments in the pregnancy and birth that were a little stressful, but nothing outside the norm.

In our eyes, many parents or parents to be struggle throughout the pregnancy, during and after birth. This just wasn't us!

Essentially, we were just normal parents with everything going to plan!

So why didn't I feel right after our second child being born? I just couldn't put a finger on it.

I had spent 10 years in the Emergency Services, seeing a magnitude of trauma, death and some really quite horrible experiences. A hell of a lot more than most people! I was also a trained Mental Health First Aider!

I had been (and still am) a Health & Wellness Coach, concentrating on Fitness, Wellbeing and Mindset. I was classed as "inspirational" and a "motivational coach".

I wanted to be a professional speaker, talking to people about mental wellbeing, personal development and improving your life through your thoughts!

All in all, Mental Health related issues shouldn't affect me!

As a Firefighter and a Coach, people relied on me; I had to be strong, for them! I couldn't show my emotions. What would people think of me? I simply had to just bury these feelings and not let on.

But how could I? I didn't know how! I completely avoided things that I previously enjoyed. I hated cricket, something I was so passionate about for at least 16 years. I just wanted to work and never be at home or around my family. I despised the gym or any form of fitness, finding every excuse under the sun not to be active.

And then there were my actual feelings. Crying randomly at minor little things during the day, but never in front of anyone else! Getting completely emotional over the tiniest of details. I remember getting extremely angry over a driver cutting up another driver, with me being nowhere near involved or affected! There was just no rhyme or reason for it. I was also avoiding my friends, deliberately ignoring calls from them, not responding to personal messages for days and trying to avoid any eye contact with people walking past with a hope of not having to speak with anyone. It was just completely unlike me!

The friendly, inspirational and outgoing person, who I was before the birth, was just nowhere to be seen!

Now, I have been around Mental Health for a long long time. I have previously raised money for Mental Health Charities, I had completed a Mental Health First Aid course and I had witness people suffering from Mental Health related issues in completely different environments. I have always actively tried to help people speak about their feelings with an attitude of "a problem shared is a problem halved."

But I simply didn't take the same attitude. Why? I cannot tell you. I just don't know myself. Maybe I was in denial? Maybe I thought I could cope without anyone knowing? Maybe I was overreacting or something?

I know for certain that I am not the only one who's ever felt like this. I know for certain people have been in the same situation as me and I know for certain that others have been reluctant to talk to someone.

But it still didn't stop the fact that people around me, being so happy and saying "you must be delighted", "Many Congratulations" and "how great a feeling it is to be a dad again!"

I couldn't tell people I didn't feel like this. I didn't want to burst other people's bubble, or be the bearer of bad news or tell people that I am struggling. All I remember saying to myself is "keep quiet, be brave and we will get through this!" I am not sure I ever believed myself!

-

So what changed?

I remember it clearly, another night where I was looking after my son alone. My wife was babysitting for another family and I just thought to myself, "I can't do this anymore." My son was constantly crying, as he wanted his mum! He just wouldn't take the bottle of formula. There was simply nothing I could do to stop him crying. I said to my daughter, who was 4 years old, "I just can't cope with this anymore." Something she then repeated further down the line to her mother!

I took my daughter to bed, leaving my son crying downstairs with his calming music on, and the first thing she said to me is "Daddy, is he going to stop crying." As a Dad, you have to say "Yes of course darling! He's just hungry!" Though I am not sure I really believed it.

After she was in bed, I went back downstairs to "face the music", my son was still crying…like he was ever going to stop in that time! I picked up my phone and messaged my wife " –Can I drop him off to you?" Obviously I got a negative response and a message back saying "Is it really that bad?!"

But that's exactly what it made me feel – I felt that maybe I was making more of this than what's really going on? The crying was still on going though!

After a few chosen swear words, a few tears and my son eventually taking the bottle, I thought to myself, something has really got to change! I cannot go on like this!

My son didn't fall asleep until his mother came home. And after a short cuddle and a little feed, he was fast asleep! Though it was nice and peaceful at last, I just felt so inadequate as a father!

I remember saying to my wife, "I can't continue like this anymore!" but I got a reply of "he's just going through something." This was clearly referring to our son having a cold or a bug rather than me going through something!

The next morning, I finally felt that I had enough. I pulled out my phone and, instead of speaking to a professional, I typed into Google "Post Natal Depression."

If anyone else has done this, you've probably got the same results as me! A whole load of different articles and information about Post Natal Depression related to Women. So many different support groups, pages about what to do with Post Natal Depression as a new mother and everything else that came with it!

I then retyped "Post Natal Depression in Men" – this was more beneficially telling me that men can get Post Natal Depression and all the signs and symptoms associated. I literally went down this listed as a checklist…Yes, Yes, Yes, Yes, Yes and so on!

It was then at that point I realised that I may be suffering. But what do I do next? Do I tell someone? Do I speak to my Doctors? Tell my wife? It just led to so many more questions.

So I just kept on reading the articles, searching for answers. The most common answer was to have a chat with my Doctors Surgery and speak to family and friends.

At this stage, this wasn't an option for me! Speaking to the Doctors would mean that it would affect my work life as a firefighter, it would be forever on my "record" and it just wasn't worth bothering them over something so trivial when they had so much more important things to deal with!

Again, speaking with family, how could I? I didn't want to show weakness, I had to be strong for them and I simply didn't want anyone to panic or worry!

But I had to do something, so I told myself to tell my wife how I was feeling!

It took me a while, I was building up the courage, I was nervous, felt uncomfortable and had no idea what the reaction was going to be! But I just had to do it! So I did...

If I'm going to be honest, it really didn't come out the way I wanted. I remember telling my wife how I felt and that things were just too much. I got a reply of "Well maybe you are just doing too much?"

This was not the answer I was looking for or the reply I wanted! This actually made me feel worse! Why would I stop doing the things I enjoy most and that were going to give us a future?!

I don't blame my wife for her reply, though it did take me some time to really understand it. As a Mum, her main focus is to make sure the kids are looked after. It's a natural thing for Mothers – it's instinct. And talking about Mental Health is still not really a common thing in these days! So I guess it was just one of those things.

I wasn't feeling any better though! I had no answers, no clear way out and my wife continued to do babysitting leaving me with my kids at home alone all over again!

It was then a phone call that changed everything for me. I was flicking through my phone and one of my best friends & business partner started FaceTime calling me. I had been ignoring his calls for a while and I only answered it by accident! But after I accepted the call, I felt I had to speak with him.

During the call, after telling him that I felt great and that I had been rushed off my feet due to the new baby and that's why I hadn't been too active in my business, I was asked one simple question, "Is everything ok bro?"

This was all I needed to say how I was really feeling! I explained how I was really feeling and I that I thought I had Post Natal Depression. It all just came out in one blurb, I didn't really know what I said but I heard what I needed to hear, "I am here for you bro, we all are!" (This was referring to our team, our community)

This was honestly like a weight lifted off my shoulders, I felt relief! It was nice that someone else knew what I was going through and that I had somewhere there who would listen to me if needed!

It wasn't till a couple of weeks later I spoke to another friend. A very close family friend who I had known since the day they were born. We met up for a drink and had a great chat about all sorts of different things. It was a conversation full of excitement and joy. But again a simple question came, "Is everything ok with you?"

This was then enough for me to really say what was going on. I just told everything!

My friend had their own troubles previously and was more than happy to share experiences and coping mechanisms.

It was the biggest relief! What I was experiencing was completely natural, it made sense and I wasn't alone.

I was given lots of great advice on what to do, how to cope and who to speak if I needed to.

The only way to describe it is that it was like a massive weighted vest being lifted off my shoulders and my back. It was such a relief!

So what helped me get back on track? Well, I'll cover these different topics in greater detail throughout this book.

The First action I took was to get counselling. I wasn't really interested at first and really didn't think I needed help! But a friend said "why don't you just try it?"

That was enough for me to give it a go. I was fortunate enough to have access to The Fire Fighters Charity, who were able to provide me some counselling to help me recover. I'll go into more detail about my experience in later chapters, however it certainly helped me start to process things!

Recovery starts within! I had been exposed to Personal Development previously; it was something that had already changed my life for the better. I needed it now more than ever! Changing your Mindset really will Change your Life!

Looking at things in a positive way was only the first step in the journey. It certainly wasn't a complete fix but it definitely helped!

Understanding my Mindset, the Mindset of people around me and how I can choose the people that surround me (and effectively the thoughts around me). This is an integral part of the process. Again, you can control your thoughts and you can control the people you spend your time with, which therefore allows you to control your environment.

This is all well and good, but where on Earth do you start? Again, a question that I asked myself! My advice, dive with both feet in and just go for it! Take action more than planning on how you are going to do something.

Just start, find a book, find a course, find something that is going to help you! You will soon work out what you like, what you dislike and most importantly, what is working!

Since this challenging time in my life, I have been so open to talk about my journey. Why?! Simply because there are so many others who have been or are struggling with Mental Health Issues and especially Post Natal Depression.

Men, especially, are living in silence and just struggling on with the pains and difficulties of Mental Health Issues. I want to help inspire other men to reach out and to seek support and assistance through their journey. You do not need to suffer in silence!

Writing this book is the first step in the process. I know for sure that someone in this world will pick up this book and it'll positively impact his or her life! That gives me the strength to make an even bigger impact on this world!

RICH WHARTON

Mental Health

Disclaimer – I am not an Expert in Mental Health and don't portray myself to be. I am simply providing my own views on the subject

We've all heard about Mental Health and more commonly the Issues associated with Mental Health.

In my opinion, everyone has Mental Health, Good and Bad! This is also referred to as your mood. We go through waves in our days and our lives of feeling good and bad. Mental Health issues come when you are either at the extremes of these moods or you are in a prolonged state of one of these moods.

Mental Health can come in all different forms; anxiety, depression, Post Traumatic Stress Disorder, Stress, Illness, Disease...there are so many more! There isn't a League Table defining which is worse than the others, people experience them differently and just deal or try to deal with them differently. They can come in all different forms and there can be all sorts of different triggers!

I often see people brand others who are suffering Mental Health Issues. For instance, some people see people suffering as "stuck for life" or like it's a terminal illness. This is completely INCORRECT!

I personally compare Mental Health Issues to a broken leg. Firstly, it's a temporary thing – it will get better and repair! You may need help and assistance in the process of repair, but it can get there. Secondly, it is not forever! I feel some people see it as a stamp that cannot be removed once you have suffered; again, I disagree with this and feel that you can 'repair' back to a well state. It also never totally leaves you, something or someone can trigger a response. I recognise that serious illness and disease may be irreversible but professional support and treatment can help.

I will say, however, that you will not return back to yourself before you suffered from Mental Health issues. Reason being is that your awareness and experiences have given you greater exposure and you cannot take that away. On the other side, I feel that this can give you a positive advantage in your own awareness on how to cope with future experiences and help those that you know who may be suffering.

There is huge stigma that surrounds Mental Health, and though we are massively improving in this field, there is still huge work to be done! We are all part of this, we can all help raise awareness and create a culture where we all feel we can speak to one another!

Post Natal Depression

**Information taken from the PANDAS Foundation website - https://pandasfoundation.org.uk/what-is-pnd/post-natal-depression/ **

Postnatal depression (PND) is a common problem that occurs after pregnancy and affects more than 1 in 10 women within a year of giving birth. It can also affect dads and partners. PND can present itself in different ways, and many parents don't realise they have the condition because it can develop gradually over time.

What are the symptoms?

- Low mood and persistent sadness
- Lack of energy
- Difficulty bonding with baby
- Overeating and under eating for comfort
- Frightening and intrusive thoughts
- Lack of enjoyment and loss of interest in the wider world
- Trouble sleeping at night and feeling sleepy during the day
- Withdrawing from contact with other people
- Lack of concentration and difficulty making decisions

Causes

The cause of postnatal depression isn't completely clear but it has been associated with the following factors:

- A history of mental health problems earlier in life or during pregnancy
- A lack of support from close family or friends
- A poor relationship with your partner
- A recent stressful event, such as bereavement

Postnatal depression is different to the 'baby blues', which last up to two weeks after giving birth. If you continue to feel down, tearful or anxious beyond this time, you could have PND.

◆ ◆ ◆

For me, I only understood that I had things from my past affecting me after I started counselling. Things were brought up in my counselling that I thought would never affect me at all! They were so small and insignificant in my life that I simply just dismissed them, but they came up through my sessions.

I didn't really know what to make of counselling when I was offered it. I knew the stigma behind counselling and wanted to keep it a secret to everyone! Even my counsellor said; *"What do you want to get out of these sessions?"* My Answer, *"I don't really know?!"*

Throughout my counselling, it really helped me park things and understand circumstances in my life. The best way I can describe the way I felt before and after counselling is that before, it was just like a block of flats and more specifically the post room of that block of flats. Instead of all the post being placed into the correct boxes, the post was simply dropped on the floor. This is manageable for a period of time, but then builds up to an unmanageable level. When my son was born, this was the "straw that broke the camel's back." It was the trigger that meant I couldn't cope anymore!

Counselling simply helped me process that information, or in the post room point of view, start putting the post in the right boxes. The little things that were playing on my mind could get filed away and allow me to park them. This isn't a "fix" but it really helped me process everything that was going in my mind to a manageable level.

My personal views, and I mentioned this last chapter, are that we all have mental health. Some days it is good. Some days it's not so good. We can feel sad and upset without it being brandished as mental health issues. The most important thing is to understand and appreciate your mental health and how it fluctuates. If you can read how you're feeling then you can deal with how you are feeling. My only advice is to not "brush it under the carpet", or in other words, forget about it!

LIFE BEHIND THE MASK

Friends & Family

Would you want someone you love feel like they can reach out to you when they are struggling? Of course!

Me too! So when I felt that I couldn't speak to my family then that was so tough for me!

I still haven't spoken about all my challenges and suffering with loved ones or family. This was especially hard with the idea of talking to my "Traditional" Parents. What would they say?!

I had heard previously of people talking about Mental Health as a "weakness" or "attention-seeking" and I just couldn't be brandished with this. But not telling people, especially family members, then feels like you are lying to them!

I avoided saying anything for weeks. I was trying to find the perfect time and the perfect moment and the perfect way to tell them. I remember telling myself that no matter how long I waited, the moment will never be perfect!

It was actually one day when my parents came to visit. We had a lovely afternoon chatting like everything was ok. It wasn't until they were about to walk out the door when I said something. I felt like I had a massive build up of emotions and feelings and just blurted out with it. I was incredibly nervous!

The response I got was even more interesting! My parents pretty much said "we know" and said they sensed something was troubling me. Their only question was "why didn't you tell us?"

This was actually a question I asked myself. Why didn't I tell my parents? It was that easy to think after I had told them. I just said, "I felt I couldn't". Again, more questions came as to why I felt I couldn't and in all honesty, I just couldn't explain it!

This was exactly the same when I spoke to my brother. I couldn't explain why I couldn't tell him why I felt like this.

I think both my parents and my brother felt a bit hurt by the fact I couldn't come to them. The 3 people in my life who have ALWAYS been there for me, who I've grown up with all my life and the people I could trust most.

But maybe that was the reason why I couldn't tell them? Could it be the fact that it might hurt them? Or will they constantly worry about me? I just didn't want to explore that, give them that burden or worry.

I then thought to myself that if someone I love or close to couldn't come to me with their feelings then that would also hurt me.

I knew from this moment on that I always wanted to talk about my feelings, my emotions and my Mental Health. I always want to talk about my experiences with Mental health Issues in a way to help inspire others to talk, to allow an environment where other's feel they can talk and to make talking about Mental Health related issues and common place in society.

In my opinion, I won't be able to help everyone. But if I can help at least one person then I have done my job! That person may then go on to help one person and so on! Over time, this will have a greater impact of generations inspiring the next generation to talk about Mental Health until it is common practice.

In my time, I have seen greater impacts being made by society. The introduction of Mental Health First Aiders, positive impacts by companies to recognise and promote Mental Health and the amount of awareness going into talking, it is just a start but I feel it is our responsibility to continue this journey!

RICH WHARTON

Personal Development

I will only touch very briefly on Personal Development:

1) Because it's a huge topic
2) Because I am writing a book solely on the topic!

The thing is with personal development is that it is very different for everyone! You cannot just recommend a book or a course and it'll be a fix. Essentially, you have to try and test the waters yourself to see what works and what doesn't.

I have tried reading books, listening to audiobooks, meditation, attending courses, online courses, daily tricks and so on... I like to think I am fairly seasoned in the personal development bracket.

Has it helped??? Yes massively! But it isn't the only thing that helps.

Personal Development needs to be blended in with life and that's the only way things can improve. It's the first stepping-stone to encourage you to try and essentially fail! I know how it sounds – why would you want me to fail?!

Well, the failure leads to learning and the learning leads to success. This is exactly the same for your Mental Health. You have to learn how to fail first before you learn how to make things better.

The best thing about it is once you've been through an experience, you are now experienced! So you know how to cope (or not cope) with a situation if it happens again!

My personal favourite with personal development is audiobooks. The reason being is that they are easy to digest, you are not being disturbed as you might if reading a book, you can listen to it anywhere, say in the car or on a train or cooking, and they are fairly cheap! It's a great place to start to dip your toe in the water.

The courses can be really good. I've been on a couple cheaper ones – but they do jump in price for the really well known ones! I have heard some incredible things about these courses. Definitely worth it, if you have the money!

Meditation is an interesting one. Now, I wasn't the biggest fan of meditation before I tried practising. I just couldn't understand how sitting in silence on your own with your eyes shut could ever help…but when you do actually try, it completely changes your mind!

I am going to be honest here; it's not always the easiest! Some days I just cannot sit still, I fidget and it annoys me more than it helps! Other days, I just don't want it to end! They call meditation a "practice" because it really is that! You don't always get it right and it does take time to master – but it's worth persevering with and the benefits can be incredible!

Whatever it is that you attempt, just give it a good go! Whether it being a book, course or meditation, whatever it is – just be consistent with it for at least a month! Things will not miraculously change overnight by doing something once. It will take time, as I mentioned previously, it's a healing process. See what works for you and just persist with it. If it's still not working after a month, then stop and try something else.

If you would like to explore more about personal development and my thoughts and feelings towards growth, please check out my book on Personal Development!

LIFE BEHIND THE MASK

Feeling Good

I would have called this section "Be Selfish" but I chose not to in case it put people off. Being selfish is often branded as a negative word/phrase and people think it's wrong to be selfish.

I disagree; I think we need to be more selfish. We need to look after ourselves and feel good! I believe we should do more things for ourselves and go and enjoy our life!

I stopped pretty much everything that I enjoyed when I was suffering. My cricket disappeared, I stopped seeing friends, I constantly worked to hide my troubles and my relationship with my wife just disappeared.

What I really needed to do was to go and do something fun, something that challenged me or something that gave me joy!

I actually started doing this on my road to recovery – I became a Stand-Up Comedian! Well, I did a course and started giving it a go. I definitely haven't got a TV Special or appeared at the World's biggest arenas!

This did however give me some joy and excitement in my life. It also challenged me and took me out of my comfort zone! Standing on stage is something I've been used to, as a speaker, I've done this regularly. But telling jokes is a completely new one on me! This was scary, I would think, "What if people don't laugh?!". But the best thing about it was that it made me smile and laugh, and helped me bring joy back into my life!

Exercises and sport is another good one to get involved with – something I stopped when I was struggling! Doing exercise releases endorphins in your body, a hormone that essentially makes you feel good! It actually makes you feel more awake, alive and energetic! And if you cannot just get on with running, cycling or the gym, then maybe some group exercise classes are for you? Or trying a new sport? Team sports and doing exercises within a community is a fantastic way to meet new friends and get that endorphin rush at the same time! Gardening has also helped many people, you can make it as strenuous or relaxed as you want plus have the benefit of seeing things grow - hopefully!

Other things you can try could be creative activities, like my Stand Up Comedy! Maybe painting or music or something along those lines might be an idea? You can even do some of these things at home, though getting out of the house in a new environment can do the world of good!

Now, one thing you are probably thinking " –what will my partner think if I am spending time doing new activities and exercise?" I guess you are thinking this because it is exactly what I was thinking! And I get it, it'll be hard to initially talk about this to a partner to 'get permission' to attend. My advice is to be open and honest as to why you are wanting to, it'll help with the conversations about mental health too, and secondly, allow time for your partner to do the same!

Doing exercise and activities together are extremely beneficial, this is something that is easier said than done though! With a new born baby (and possibly other children) going out as a couple to do something new seems near impossible. Definitely leverage off family and friends if you can. Get a baby sitter. It will really really help! Obviously, this won't be possible when your child is really little, but after about 6 months or so then this is a great option!

In the early stages, maybe a walk in the park as a couple with the pram might be something to do, even if you don't feel like it. It's amazing how conversation flows when you walk and you can really open up to talk about your feelings. The fresh air will also do you good and brings you closer to nature too.

Whatever you chose to do, you need to dedicate that time for yourself. How can you help someone else if you can't help yourself?

It absolutely is ok to be selfish! You are looking after yourself and it's vital that you do!

Charities & Support Partners

PANDAS Foundation – https://www.pandasfoundation.org.uk/

MIND – https://www.mind.org.uk/

Samaritans – https://www.samaritans.org/

The Fire Fighters Charity - https://www.firefighterscharity.org.uk/

NHS Mental Health Services - https://www.nhs.uk/nhs-services/mental-health-services/

Mental Health Foundation - https://www.mentalhealth.org.uk/

Henri Saha Individual & Business Support Coaching - https://henrisaha.com/

Mike Pagan "Mental Wealth" - https://mikepagan.com/

Rethink - https://www.rethink.org/

Calm - https://www.calm.com/

There are many more about there which can be found via the Internet.

LIFE BEHIND THE MASK

ABOUT THE AUTHOR

Richard Wharton

A Proud Dad of 2, a dedicated Husband, a Firefighter and a Health & Wellness Coach, Richard has always been loving and caring. He has a genuine love of helping people and this is why he wrote this book.

Richard has always had a passion for Speaking, helping provide value to others and making other people's lives better! If you have an engagement you'd like Rich to speak at then please contact him viat the details below:

https://www.linkedin.com/in/rich-wharton

Printed in Great Britain
by Amazon